PARALYMPICS

THE STORY OF CANADIANS

IN THE OLYMPIC WINTER GAMES

Written by Blaine Wiseman

Weigl

Published by Weigl Educational Publishers Limited
6325 10 Street SE
Calgary, Alberta
T2H 2Z9

www.weigl.com

Library and Archives Canada Cataloguing in Publication data available upon request.
Fax 403-233-7769 for the attention of the Publishing Records department.

ISBN 978-1-55388-941-0 (hard cover)
ISBN 978-1-55388-950-2 (soft cover)

Printed in the United States of America
1 2 3 4 5 6 7 8 9 0 13 12 11 10 09

Editor: Heather C. Hudak
Design: Terry Paulhus

All of the Internet URLs given in the book were valid at the time of publication. However, due to the dynamic nature of the Internet, some addresses may have changed, or sites may have ceased to exist since publication. While the author and publisher regret any inconvenience this may cause readers, no responsibility for any such changes can be accepted by either the author or the publisher.

Every reasonable effort has been made to trace ownership and to obtain permission to reprint copyright material. The publishers would be pleased to have any errors or omissions brought to their attention so that they may be corrected in subsequent printings.

Weigl acknowledges Getty Images as its primary image supplier for this title.

We gratefully acknowledge the financial support of the Government of Canada through the Book Publishing Industry Development Program (BPIDP) for our publishing activities.

Contents

What are the Paralympics?

The Paralympic Games are a sports competition for athletes with disabilities. Like the Olympics, the Paralympics celebrate the athletic achievements of its competitors. The games are held in the same year as the Olympics, and since the summer games in Seoul, South Korea, in 1988, and the winter games in Albertville, France, in 1992, they have been held in the same city as the Olympic Games.

The idea of a sports competition for disabled athletes first came about in 1948. That year, Sir Ludwig Guttmann, a doctor in England, organized a sporting event for World War II veterans who had suffered **spinal cord** injuries. Guttmann used the competition as part of a **rehabilitation** program for his patients and invited patients from other hospitals around England to compete in the games. The competition took place in Stoke Mandeville, England, the same year the Olympic Games took place in London. Four years later, competitors from Holland joined Guttmann's games.

In 1960, Guttmann brought together 400 wheelchair athletes from 23 countries to Rome, Italy, where the Summer Olympic Summer Games were taking place. There, they became the first Paralympians. Today, about 4,000 athletes from more than 130 countries compete in the Paralympic Games.

In 1976, at the Paralympic Summer Games in Toronto, Ontario, **visually impaired** athletes and **amputees** were included in the games. Since then, other disability groups have been added. Today, each athlete is classed under one of six disability groups, including amputee, **cerebral palsy**, visual impairment, spinal cord injuries, **intellectual disability**, and a group for other disabilities. The groups apply to different sports and make the competition more equal for all competitors in each sport.

WINTER PARALYMPICS
HOST CITIES

CITY	YEAR
Örnsköldsvik, Sweden	1976
Geilo, Norway	1980
Innsbruck, Austria	1984
Innsbruck, Austria	1988
Albertville, France	1992
Lillehammer, Norway	1994
Nagano, Japan	1998
Salt Lake City, United States	2002
Turin, Italy	2006
Vancouver, Canada	2010

VANCOUVER 2010

SALT LAKE CITY 2002

✷ **CANADIAN TIDBIT** Vancouver is the second Canadian city to host the Paralympic Games. Toronto hosted the Summer Games in 1976.

Paralympic Sports

Many sports appear in both the Paralympics and the Olympics, such as swimming, alpine skiing, and **biathlon**. The Paralympics, however, also feature unique sports, such wheelchair basketball, goalball, and ice sledge hockey. Currently, there are five Winter Paralympic sports. These are alpine skiing, cross-country skiing, biathlon, ice sledge hockey, and wheelchair curling.

Alpine Skiing   Biathlon   Cross-Country Skiing   Ice Sledge Hockey   Wheelchair Curling

ÖRNSKÖLDSVIK 1976

LILLEHAMMER 1994

GEILO 1980

TURIN 2006

INNSBRUCK 1984/1988

ALBERTVILLE 1992

NAGANO 1998

Canada and the Paralympics

Canada first participated in the Paralympics during the 1968 games in Tel Aviv, Israel. Canadian athletes, including Hilda May Torok Binns and Eugene Reimer, won a total of 19 medals at the games, including six gold medals. Binns won gold medals in the 60-metre wheelchair dash and the 25-metre freestyle swimming event, as well as the silver medal in the wheelchair slalom race. Reimer won gold medals in the men's club throw and **discus** events, and a silver in the **javelin**.

Binns and Reimer competed for Canada again at the 1972 Paralympics in Heidelberg, Germany. With three more medals each, they helped the Canadian team earn another 19 medals. This time, Binns won two silver medals and one bronze. Reimer won another two gold medals, repeating in the discus and winning the **pentathlon** while helping the Canadian wheelchair relay team win a silver medal. Doug Bovee of Edmonton, Alberta, also won three medals—one gold, one silver, and one bronze.

The 1976 Paralympic Games in Toronto were historic for a number of reasons. The inclusion of people with disabilities other than spinal cord injuries led to new events at the games, including goalball and high jump. As well, the games were televised for the first time and broadcast around southern Ontario.

Goalball is a sport played by athletes who are visually impaired. In this sport, the ball makes noise, helping blind athletes locate it.

The high jump in the Paralympics is an acknowledgement of the astounding feats that are performed by Paralympians.

Wheelchair racing, also called athletics, was first introduced into the Paralympics in 1960.

At the 1998 Winter Paralympics in Nagano, Japan, Canada's Daniel Gary Wesley won gold in the Men's Super G LW11 Class.

Audiences watched in person and on television as 18-year-old Canadian Arnie Boldt became the star athlete. Boldt, who had an amputated leg, won gold medals in the high jump and long jump events. He was honoured as the outstanding athlete of the games. That year, Canada won a total of 77 medals.

The first Winter Paralympics took place in 1976 in Örnsköldsvik, Sweden. Events were held in alpine and nordic skiing. Canada won four medals. Lorna Manzer earned three of those, including gold in 5-kilometre cross country skiing. John Gow won Canada's other medal, taking home the gold in men's slalom.

Canada has continued to compete at a high level at both the Summer and Winter Paralympics, consistently placing in the top 10 countries. At the 2006 Paralympic Winter Games in Turin, Italy, Canadian athletes won a total of 13 medals, including gold in ice sledge hockey and wheelchair curling. In 2008, at the Summer Paralympic Games in Beijing, China, Canada won 50 medals. At those games, Chantal Petitclerc took home five gold medals in wheelchair racing.

🍁 **CANADIAN TIDBIT** The Canadian Paralympic Committee has set a goal of finishing the 2010 Paralympics as one of the top three medal-winning nations.

All The Right Equipment

All of the sports featured in the Winter Paralympics are based on sports that are also featured in the Winter Olympics. Since athletes who compete in the Paralympics are disabled, certain adaptations have been made to the way the sports are played and the equipment that is used.

The skis used by Paralympic alpine skiers have been adapted to allow them to hurtle down snow-covered hills at high speeds. Skiers who are able to use one or both of their legs use regular skis, but skiers with a physical disability affecting both of their legs use a device called a sit-ski. A sit-ski is a chair that sits atop two skis and is used for both alpine and nordic skiing. Paralympics alpine skiers use poles that are the same length as regular ski poles but have small skis attached to the bottom instead of spikes. These poles, called outriggers, help the skiers keep their balance.

Ice sledge hockey players use a type of sled instead of hockey skates. These sleds have two blades on the bottom that allow the puck to pass underneath. Ice sledge hockey players push themselves along the ice using two small hockey sticks. The sticks have a spike on one end and a blade on the other. Players dig the spike into the ice to push themselves forward. They use the blade to control the puck, similar to a hockey stick.

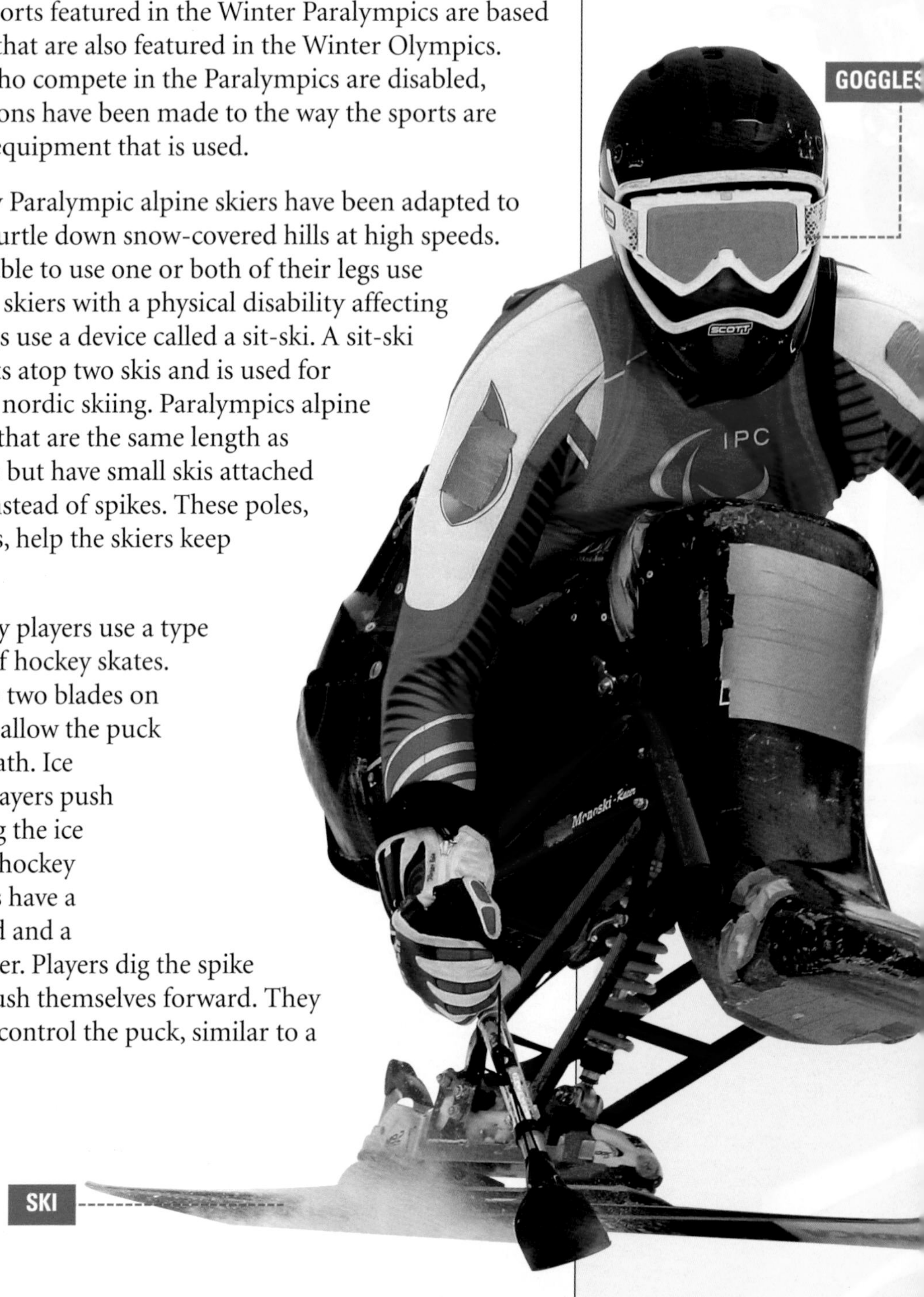

GOGGLES

SKI

Wheelchair curling entered the Paralympics in 2006. The game is played in manner similar to other forms of curling. Athletes with lower body disabilities sit in wheelchairs as they curl rocks down the rink.

Visually impaired athletes can compete in the biathlon at the Paralympics. This sport features cross-country skiing and target shooting. Competitors ski a certain distance before using an adapted rifle to shoot targets. The rifle has a receiver that picks up a frequency from a transmitter in the centre of the target. As the biathlete aims at the target, it makes a sound. The sound becomes more high pitched as the athlete aims closer to the centre of the target. This allows visually impaired athletes to use their ears, rather than their eyes, to find the target.

In alpine skiing events, skiers wear goggles to keep ice and snow from flying into their eyes. They also wear hard shell helmets to protect their head.

Skiers must use the correct gear to help protect them as they glide across the snow or ice as fast as possible.

AERODYNAMIC SUIT

OUTRIGGER

🍁 **CANADIAN TIDBIT** Doug Bovee won three Paralympic medals in 1972 while racing in a three-wheeled wheelchair designed by Canadian Dr. Robert Steadward.

Qualifying to Compete

Skiers must meet or beat the qualifying times set for each event in order to make the nation's Olympic team.

Paralympians are high performance athletes who must meet very challenging criteria in order to qualify for the Paralympic games. Athletes must be elite performers on the world stage in their sport, competing against other athletes from all over the world and within their own country.

There are only a certain number of positions available to Canadians in each Paralympic sport, so athletes must be the best in Canada in their sport. Each country is limited to 30 alpine skiers, 23 nordic skiers, one sledge hockey team, and one wheelchair curling team. Competitors must qualify for the Games and be chosen to represent their country.

In order to compete in the Paralympics, athletes must compete in qualifying events, such as world championships. Athletes must perform at a high level at these events and achieve certain time limits set by the international federation governing their sport.

Skiers qualify for the Paralympics by achieving certain limits set by the International Ski Federation (FIS). Once skiers have met FIS qualifying standards, the Canadian Paralympic ski team can choose them for the team.

For ice sledge hockey players to compete for Canada, they must demonstrate their skill, passion, and commitment to the sport. Of all the sledge hockey players in Canada, only 18 are chosen for the Canadian sledge hockey team.

In both qualifying and competitive races, the visually impaired skier competes with a sighted guide through the racecourses.

Racers can reach speeds of more than 100 kilometres per hour in Paralympic alpine skiing races.

Disability Groups

Each Paralympic event is broken into disability groups and classifications. Athletes are classified according to the nature and severity of their disability. Athletes who have lost part of their eyesight, for example, are classed differently than athletes that have completely lost their eyesight. In the same manner, double-leg amputees are classified differently than single-leg amputees. Athletes in each group compete against other athletes in the same event with the same classification. For example, visually impaired biathletes compete against other visually impaired biathletes.

Alpine skiing

Visual impairment, amputees

Nordic skiing

Visual impairment, amputees, spinal cord injuries, cerebral palsy, other physical disabilities

Wheelchair curling

Lower body physical disabilities: amputees, spinal cord injuries, cerebral palsy, other physical disabilities affecting the legs or lower body

Ice sledge hockey

Lower body physical disabilities: amputees, spinal cord injuries, cerebral palsy, other physical disabilities affecting the legs or lower body

Australia's Cameron Rahles Rahbula of Australia competes in the men's giant slalom event.

Paralympic Sports

Ice sledge hockey is a sport for athletes with lower body disabilities. It was invented in Sweden in the early 1960s by hockey players who wanted to keep playing the sport even though they were disabled. Most ice sledge hockey rules are the same as those used to play ice hockey. Each team has six members on the ice at one time. This includes five players and one goaltender. The objective of the game is to put the puck in the other team's net. Ice sledge hockey is a very fast, physical sport. Full body contact is allowed, meaning players can crash into each other at high speeds. For this reason, players must wear protective equipment, including helmets and pads. Since joining the Paralympics in 1994, ice sledge hockey has become one of the most popular sports. In 2010, women will be able to take part in Paralympic ice sledge hockey for the first time.

Wheelchair curling is similar to curling, only competitors sit in wheelchairs. The goal is to throw a rock down a sheet of ice, or rink, sliding it as close as possible to a centre target. In curling, sweeping the ice to guide the rock is a major part of the game. Wheelchair curlers do not sweep. This means that players cannot control the speed and direction of the rock by manipulating the ice around it. Wheelchair curlers must rely on the accuracy of their rock-throwing skills to gain points.

Alpine skiing is one of the most popular sports in both the Paralympics and Olympics. This sport is made up of several events, including downhill, slalom, giant slalom, super giant slalom, and super combined. Each event features one skier at a time racing down a snowy hill. Skiers must pass through a series of gates along the way. There can be as many as 75 gates in a downhill event. If competitors miss a set of gates, they are disqualified from the race. Skiers reach speeds of more than 100 kilometres per hour on hills that combine turns and jumps.

Ice sledge hockey is the Paralympic version of ice hockey. Players use specialized sledges and sticks to propel themselves and the puck around the ice surface.

🍁 **CANADIAN TIDBIT** The Canadian wheelchair curling and ice sledge hockey teams hope to win their second straight gold medals in 2010. No other country has won two gold medals in a row in these sports.

Nordic skiing consists of biathlon and cross-country events. In cross-country skiing, athletes race against each other and the clock. The goal is to finish the race in the shortest time possible. **Stamina** and strength are two very important parts of cross country skiing.

Skiers race as far as 20 kilometres across flat land, hills, and rolling terrain.

Biathlon competitors carry a rifle strapped to their back while they ski.

It takes tremendous skill to maneuver the sharp turns around the gates in the slalom event.

A Paralympic biathlon trail is 3.75 or 5 kilometres long. At certain places along the trail, biathletes stop to shoot targets. They stop to shoot twice for short-distance biathlons and four times for long-distance biathlons. It can be a challenge to shoot straight when competitors are tired and breathing heavily. Biathletes must be able to relax their breathing so that they can shoot straight. They are judged on a combination of how fast they finish the course and how accurately they shoot.

PERFORMANCE ENHANCING DRUGS

Although the Paralympics are a celebration of excellence and sportsmanship, some athletes use performance enhancing drugs to give them an unfair advantage over other athletes. There are many different types of performance enhancing drugs, including steroids. Some make muscles bigger, others help muscles recover more quickly, while some can make athletes feel less pain, giving them more **endurance**. The International Olympic Committee (IOC) takes the use of performance enhancing drugs very seriously. Regular testing of athletes helps ensure competitors do not use drugs to unnaturally improve their skills. Paralympic sports require a mixture of strength, speed, and endurance. Many performance enhancing drugs will help an athlete in one of these areas, but hurt them in others. For example, a drug may cause the heart to pump more blood to muscles in the arms, making the athlete physically stronger. This takes blood away from the heart and lungs, giving the athlete less endurance and slower long-term recovery. There are serious mental and physical health problems that arise from using these drugs, such as sleep problems, sickness, and high blood pressure. Athletes who use steroids for a long time may die early from heart attacks and other problems.

Exploring the Venue

One venue for the 2010 Paralympics is the Thunderbird Arena in Vancouver.

Paralympic events are held in the same venues as the Olympics. If the host city does not already have suitable facilities, new ones are constructed. The venues can cost more than $1 billion to build and can be used to exhibit one or multiple events.

The UBC Thunderbird Arena at the University of British Columbia in Vancouver has been renovated to host the Olympics and Paralympic Games, including the ice sledge hockey tournament. Originally, the arena had one ice rink. The building has been extended to add two more rinks. One of the new rinks will have seating for 7,200 people.

CEREMONIES

Two of the most-anticipated and popular events of the Olympics are the opening and closing ceremonies. These events are traditionally held in the largest venue that an Olympic host city can offer. Facilities such as football, baseball, or soccer stadiums are often used for these events. At the 2008 Olympic Games in Beijing, more than 90,000 people attended the opening ceremonies. The ceremonies are spectacular displays that include music, dancing, acrobatic stunts, and fireworks. The theme of the ceremonies usually celebrates the history and culture of the host nation and city. All of the athletes participating in the Olympics march into the stadium during the ceremonies. The athletes

wave their country's flag, and celebrate the achievement of competing in the Olympics.

Wheelchair curling made its Paralympic debut at the 2006 Paralympic Games in Turin.

Wheelchair curling will take place at the Vancouver Olympic/Paralympic Centre. Seating 6,000 spectators, this new building holds several curling ice sheets, an ice hockey rink, a library, a swimming centre, and a gymnasium. The building will act as a community centre after the Games end.

Biathlon and cross-country skiing events will take place at the Whistler Olympic/Paralympic Park. The 5-kilometre standing course and 3.75-kilometre sit-ski course use parts of trails that have been specially constructed for the Olympic competitions. A portable rifle range can be moved on to the courses for biathlon events.

The Whistler Creekside venue can hold 6,000 spectators. This site will be used for all Olympic and Paralympic alpine skiing competitions. The pre-existing venue was improved for the Winter Games. Men's competitions will take place on the Dave Murray Downhill slope, while women's events will be held on Franz's Run. After the games, Whistler Creekside will be used as a recreational ski hill, a training centre for the Canadian alpine ski team, and a competition venue for international events.

🍁 **CANADIAN TIDBIT** The Olympic Stadium in Montreal is one of the most expensive stadiums ever built. By the time it was paid off in 2006, the building cost more than $1.4 billion.

Sit-ski

- Alpine sit-skiers typically use a single, wide ski, called a mono ski. Nordic sit-skiers use two narrower skis that are sometimes called bi-skis. The wider base of a bi-ski provides greater stability but less maneuverability.
- Higher-quality sit-skis have sophisticated **suspension** systems between the seat and the ski. The suspension system absorbs the impact of rough terrain and jumps, improving control and comfort for the skier.
- Sit-skis can be ordered custom-made to fit the height, weight, and ability of the skier.

Wheelchair Curling

- Standard wheelchairs can be, and often are, used in wheelchair curling. The rules of the sport state that the curler's feet must not touch the ice while throwing and that the wheels of the chair must remain in contact with the ice at all times.
- Wheelchair curlers often use a rod or cue, called a delivery stick, to push their rocks. The same rod must be used for the entire competition, and it cannot give any sort of **mechanical advantage.**
- Some wheelchair curlers are able to brace themselves to remain motionless while throwing a rock. The rules permit a teammate to brace the curler while he or she is throwing but not to provide any other assistance.

Ice Sledge Hockey

- Ice sledges are made from aluminum or steel. Both metals are fairly lightweight and strong.
- Sledges sit on tempered-steel skate blades that are 3 millimetres wide. In order to let the puck move freely among the players, sledge blades cannot be longer than one-third the total length of the sledge, and the sledge must sit 8.5 to 9.5 centimetres above the ice.

- Players use two hockey sticks to move and handle the puck. Sticks must be under 1 metre in length, with a blade less than 25 centimetres long, though the goaltender's sticks may have a 35-centimetre blade. Sticks may be wood, plastic, or metal.
- Each stick has a spiked section called a pick. The pick has a minimum of six teeth that can be no longer than 4 millimetres each. The pick is used to grip the ice to allow players to propel their sledges.

Olympic Legends

PARALYMPIC MEDALS WON

1 Gold

Chris Daw

Chris Daw worked at his Paralympic dream of winning a medal for 25 years before it came true in 2006. Daw competed in wheelchair racing at the Paralympic Summer Games in 1984 in Los Angeles, California, and in 1988 in Seoul, South Korea. Daw has also competed for Canada in wheelchair basketball and marathon. He later began playing wheelchair rugby, and quickly joined the Canadian national team. Daw competed in rugby at the 2000 Summer Paralympics in Sydney, Australia. That year, he earned a spot in the bronze medal final. Daw and his teammates lost to New Zealand, a powerful rugby nation, by a score of 44 to 32. Again, Daw switched sports and began concentrating on wheelchair curling. At his first Paralympic Winter Games in 2006, Daw realized his dream. As the skip, or leader, of Team Canada, he won the first Paralympic curling gold medal. Canada won on the last shot of the match.

PARALYMPIC MEDALS WON

22 Gold   3 Silver   2 Bronze

Ragnhild Myklebust

Ragnhild Myklebust retired from Paralympic competition after the 2002 Games in Salt Lake City, at the age of 58. In her career, she won a total of 27 medals, including 22 gold medals. Myklebust has won more medals than any other athlete in the Paralympics or Olympics. She has won medals in cross-country skiing, biathlon, and ice sledge speed racing. As well, she has competed and won gold medals in every Paralympic Winter Games since 1988. In her first Games, in Innsbruck, Austria, Myklebust won five gold medals and one silver in the biathlon and cross-country skiing events. She won two more gold medals in 1992. In 1994, Myklebust won five more gold medals, two silver, and two bronze. The 1998 Games marked the third time she won five gold medals. In her final Paralympics, Myklebust had yet another five-gold-medal performance. Her domination of every event she participated in has made her the most decorated winter athlete of all time.

Reinhild Moeller

Germany's Reinhild Moeller is the most successful female Paralympic alpine skier in history. She has won a total of 13 alpine skiing medals. Eleven of these medals are gold. Competing in the standing category, Moeller has had one of her legs amputated below the knee. She has also competed in Paralympic Summer Games in wheelchair racing, winning three gold medals and one silver. In 1992 and 1994, Moeller won all four gold medals in alpine skiing. She has won Paralympic gold medals in three different decades. The last medal she won—a silver, in 2006—came 26 years after her first.

PARALYMPIC MEDALS WON

16 Gold   2 Silver   1 Bronze

Frank Hoefle

Competing in both Winter and Summer Paralympics, Frank Hoefle has won more medals than any other male Paralympian. In his career, Hoefle has won a total of 24 medals. Twenty-one of these came in the Winter Paralympics. Hoefle competed in the visually impaired categories of several sports, including road cycling and cross-country skiing. In his first appearance at the Winter Paralympics, Hoefle did not win any medals. However, in his next six appearances, he won 13 gold, five silver, and three bronze medals. Hoefle has also won one gold and two bronze medals in road cycling in his two Summer Paralympic appearances.

PARALYMPIC MEDALS WON

13 Gold   5 Silver   3 Bronze

WANT MORE?

For information about the Canadian Paralympic Committee, check out **www.paralympic.ca**.

Learn about the history of the Paralympic Games at **www.canada2010.gc.ca/101/histor/010203-eng.cfm**.

Olympic Stars

Brian McKeever

Brian McKeever, of Canmore, Alberta, hopes to become the first winter athlete to compete in both the Paralympics and Olympics. As a promising young cross-country skier, McKeever competed in the 1998 World Junior Championship, the same year that his older brother Robin competed in the Winter Olympics. Later that year, Brian was diagnosed with Stargardt's disease, a condition that causes eyesight to slowly fade. He has continued skiing and has dominated visually impaired cross-country skiing events. With Robin leading the way for the beginning parts of races, Brian takes over for the final part of the races, sprinting to the finish line. Robin creates lines in the snow that Brian can follow, and he relays information about the trail to Brian as they ski. Using this strategy, Brian has won four gold medals, two silver, and one bronze at the Paralympic Games. In 2010, Brian and Robin will compete in the Paralympics. Brian also plans to compete in the Olympics. He competed in his first able-bodied competition in 2007, finishing in 24th place. He was the top-placing Canadian in the race.

FAST FACT

Brian McKeever is the first disabled Canadian athlete to ski in an able-bodied race.

PARALYMPIC MEDALS WON

| 4 Gold | 2 Silver | 1 Bronze |

Lauren Woolstencroft

Canadian Paralympic alpine skier Lauren Woolstencroft has already competed and won at two Paralympic Winter Games. Born without legs below her knees and without her left arm below the elbow, Woolstencroft wears **prostheses** and competes in the standing category of alpine skiing. In her Paralympic debut in 2002, she won two gold medals and one bronze. At her next Paralympics, she won another gold medal and a silver. After this performance, Woolstencroft considered retiring, even though she was only in her twenties. In addition to her athletic career, Woolstencroft is an engineer working for BC Hydro, one of the main **sponsors** of the 2010 Games. As such, she has been able to prepare for the games in two ways. While training to compete, Woolstencroft has also worked on supplying light to some of the venues, including Whistler Creekside, where she will compete in four alpine skiing events.

FAST FACT

Lauren Woolstencroft was awarded the overall World Cup title, as well as the Paralympic Sport Award for best female athlete in 2007.

PARALYMPIC MEDALS WON

| 3 Gold | 1 Silver | 1 Bronze |

Colette Bourgonje

Colette Bourgonje has competed in eight Paralympic Games, including three Summer Games competitions. Bourgonje won two bronze medals in wheelchair racing at the Summer Paralympics in Barcelona, Spain, in 1992. Bourgonje won two more bronze medals at the Summer Paralympics in 1996. In 1998, she became a Paralympic legend by winning two silver medals in cross-country skiing at the Winter Paralympics in Nagano, Japan. The medals were Canada's first in Paralympic nordic skiing events. This made Bourgonje one of the only people to win multiple medals in the Summer and Winter Paralympics. In her latest Winter Paralympic Games, Bourgonje won two more bronze medals in cross-country skiing and was selected as Canada's flag bearer at the closing ceremonies. Due to her success, two streets in Saskatoon, Saskatchewan, have been named after her. Bourgonje still competes in Winter Paralympic sports and will compete in the Paralympic Winter Games in 2010.

FAST FACT

Colette Bourgonje was chosen as Saskatoon's athlete of the year in 1996 and was inducted to the Saskatoon Sport Hall of Fame in 1998.

PARALYMPIC MEDALS WON

2 Silver   2 Bronze

Paul Rosen

As the goaltender for Canada's ice sledge hockey team, Paul Rosen has a very important job. In his first appearance at the Paralympic Winter Games in 2002, Rosen and his teammates finished in fourth place. Four years of dedication by Rosen and his teammates brought them to Turin, Italy, confident in their ability to win the gold medal in 2006. Early in the tournament, Canada lost to Norway 4 to 1. The four goals by Norway were the only goals that Rosen allowed for the entire tournament. When Canada faced Norway again in the gold-medal final, Rosen would not be beaten. He made 18 saves, leading Canada to a 3 to 0 win. It was Canada's first gold medal in ice sledge hockey. Though he considered retiring after the 2006 games, Rosen decided to compete again for Canada in 2010.

FAST FACT

Paul Rosen helped the Canadian Hockey team beat Germany 5 to 0 in a semi-final match.

PARALYMPIC MEDALS WON

1 Gold

WANT MORE?

Learn more about the Paralympics at **http://archives.cbc.ca/sports/olympics/topics/1363**.

Details about Paralympic sports can be found at **www.paralympiceducation.ca/Content/home.asp**.

A Day in the Life of a Paralympic Athlete

Becoming a Paralympic athlete takes a great deal of dedication and **perseverance**. Athletes must concentrate on remaining healthy and maximizing their strength and energy. Eating special foods according to a strict schedule, taking vitamins, waking up early to train and practise, and going to bed at a reasonable hour are important parts of staying in shape for world-class athletes. All athletes have different routines and training regimens. These regimens are suited to that athlete's body and lifestyle.

Eggs are a great source of **protein** and **iron**, and are low in **calories**, making them a popular breakfast choice. A cup of orange juice is a healthy breakfast drink, while coffee can give an athlete some extra energy in the morning. A light lunch, including a sandwich, yogurt, fruit, and juice, is usually a good option. This gives the body the right amount of energy, while it is not too filling. Chicken and pasta are popular dinnertime meals.

Good nutrition is important for all athletes to enhance their performance.

Early Mornings

Paralympic athletes might wake up at 6:30 a.m. to record their resting **heart rate**. Next, they might stretch or perform yoga while their breakfast is preparing. The first exercise of the day can happen before 7:00 a.m. Depending on an athlete's sport, the exercise routine can vary. A hockey player might be in the gym lifting weights. After lifting weights for an hour, the athlete may move on to **aerobics** to help with strength and endurance.

6:30 a.m.

Morning Practice

By about 9:30 a.m. athletes are ready to practise their event. For a skier, this means putting on skis and hitting the slopes. Most Paralympic athletes have coaches and trainers who help them develop training routines. After practice, skaters stretch to keep their muscles loose and avoid injuries. Many athletes use a sauna or an ice bath to help their muscles recover quickly.

9:30 a.m.

Afternoon Nap

At about noon, many athletes choose to take a break. Sleep helps the body and mind recover from stress. After waking up at 2:00 p.m., it is time for lunch and then, more exercise. **Core** exercises help athletes with stability. Athletes use special workout equipment to exercise their cores. **Stability balls**, **medicine balls**, and **slide boards** are common pieces of equipment. Speed and quickness exercises are also important for many Paralympic athletes.

12:00 p.m.

Dinnertime

After the afternoon workout, it is dinnertime. Another healthy meal helps athletes recover from the day and prepare their body for the next day's training. The evening can be spent relaxing and doing more light stretches. It is important for athletes to rest after a hard day of training so that they can do their challenging routine again the next day.

6:00 p.m.

Paralympic Volunteers

Volunteers for the Paralympics need to be dedicated and committed in order to help make the Paralympic environment as safe as possible for the Paralympians.

Paralympic volunteers assist with snow shoveling and other tasks that will help the Paralympians to perform at their best.

Volunteers are an important part of creating an enjoyable Paralympic experience for athletes and spectators. Thousands of volunteers help organize and execute the Paralympic Games. Paralympic volunteers are enthusiastic, committed, and dedicated to helping welcome the world to the host city. Volunteers help prepare for the Paralympics in the years leading up to the events.

Before the Paralympics begin, many countries send representatives to the host city to view event venues and plans. Paralympic volunteers help make the representatives' stay enjoyable. From meeting these representatives at the airport, showing them around the city and the surrounding areas, and providing accommodations and transportation, volunteers make life easier for visitors to the host city.

CANADIAN TIDBIT About 25,000 volunteers are helping with the Olympics and Paralympics in Vancouver. They will make sure the games are a memorable, enjoyable experience for athletes, judges, spectators, and officials from all over the world.

During the Paralympics, volunteers help in many different areas. During the opening, closing, and medal ceremonies, volunteers help prepare costumes, props, and performers for the events. Editorial volunteers help by preparing written materials for use in promoting events and on the official website of the Olympics. Food and beverage volunteers provide catering services to athletes, judges, officials, spectators, and media.

Some volunteers get a chance to view events and work with competitors. Anti-doping volunteers notify athletes when they have been selected for drug testing. These volunteers explain the process to the athletes and escort them to the drug-testing facility. Other volunteers get to be involved with the sporting events by helping to maintain the venues and the fields of play, providing medical assistance to athletes, transporting athletes to events, and helping with the set-up and effective running of events.

The torch relay represents the extraordinary achievements of Paralympians, as well as their courage and determination.

Torch Relay

One of the most anticipated events of each Paralympics is the torch relay. The torch is carried along a route across the host country, until it reaches the host city during the opening ceremonies. The torch relay for 2010 covers 45,000 kilometres over 106 days. The relay will begin in Victoria before moving through communities in all 10 Canadian provinces and three territories.

About 12,000 volunteers will be chosen to carry the torch across Canada. Other volunteers help drive and maintain the vehicles that accompany the torch on its journey.

Great Paralympic Moments

Throughout the years, there have been many great moments at the Paralympic Games. At the 2006 Winter Paralympics, Chris Daw accomplished his dream of winning a gold medal for Canada, taking home the first-ever Paralympic gold medal in wheelchair curling. Despite being born without the use of his legs, Daw has been an athlete his entire life. Daw, who comes from London, Ontario, was competing in his fifth sport at his fifth Paralympic Games. After defeating Britain in the final of the curling competition, Daw and his teammates cried tears of joy as the Canadian national anthem was played in the stadium. Daw said that winning the gold medal for Canada made him so happy that, for the first time in his life, he jumped.

In 2002, at the Paralympics in Salt Lake City, Utah, Norway's Ragnhild Myklebust won her 22nd Paralympic gold medal. Myklebust accomplished this feat in the 10-kilometre women's cross-country skiing event, beating silver-medal winner Svitlana Tryfonova's adjusted time by almost one minute. This was the third time Tryfonova had come in second to Myklebust in this event. Following her win, Mykelbust said she hoped to recruit more young people to the sport.

Ice sledge hockey is traditionally a men's sport. However, women will be allowed to compete for the first time in ice sledge hockey at the 2010 Olympics.

Outriggers help three-track skiers perform effective turns.

To turn the sit-ski, skiers lean in the direction they want to turn as they drag their ski pole in the snow.

The Canadian ice sledge hockey team has competed in the Winter Paralympics since the sport was first introduced in 1994. That year, the Canadian team won a bronze medal, finishing in third place. At the following Winter Paralympics, in 1998, Canada lost to Norway in the gold-medal final, winning the silver medal. Four years later, the team hoped to take home the gold medal. After a disappointing tournament, the team finished in fourth place. However, in 2006, in Turin, Italy, the Canadian sledge hockey team faced Norway again in the final. Canada won 3 to 0, earning its first ice sledge hockey gold medal.

The sit-ski was one of the first skis developed for athletes using wheelchairs.

Paralympics and the Environment

Hosting so many people in one city can be costly to the environment. Host cities often build new venues and roads to accommodate the Games. For example, a great deal of transportation is needed to support construction projects, planning for the games, and to move the athletes, participants, volunteers, media, and spectators around the host city and its surrounding areas. This transportation causes pollution.

In recent years, the IOC and Paralympic host cities have been working to make the Paralympics more green. With their beautiful surroundings, including the Pacific Ocean to the West and the Rocky Mountains to the East, Vancouver and Whistler have taken many steps to protect the environment.

As host city of the 2010 Winter Olympics, Vancouver is taking measures to reduce harmful effects to the environment.

WHISTLER SLIDING CENTRE

At the Whistler Sliding Centre, home to the bobsleigh, luge, and skeleton events, an ice plant is used to keep the ice frozen. The heat waste from this plant is used to heat other buildings in the area. All wood waste from the Whistler sites will be chipped, composted, and reused on the same site.

LIL'WAT ABORIGINAL NATION

Working with the Lil'wat Aboriginal Nation, builders of the Paralympic cross-country ski trails created venues that could be used long after the Paralympics. About 50 kilometres of trails have been built that can be used by cross-country skiers and hikers of all skill levels.

VANCOUVER LIGHTING AND HEATING SYSTEMS

Venues in Whistler and Vancouver have been equipped with efficient lighting and heating systems. These systems reduce the amount of **greenhouse gases** released into the atmosphere during the Paralympics.

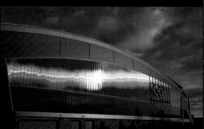

GREENHOUSE GASES

Half of the organizing committee's vehicles are either **hybrid** or equipped with fuel management technology. These vehicles emit less greenhouse gases than other vehicles. As well, venues have been made accessible to users of transit, and many event tickets include transit tickets to promote mass transportation at the games.

VANCOUVER CONVENTION AND EXHIBITION CENTRE

The Vancouver Convention and Exhibition Centre uses a seawater heating system. This system uses the surrounding natural resources to make the building a more comfortable place to visit. The centre also houses a fish habitat.

RICHMOND OLYMPIC OVAL

The Richmond Olympic Oval was built with a wooden arced ceiling. The huge amount of wood needed to build the ceiling was reclaimed from forests that have been destroyed by mountain pine beetles. These beetles feed on pine trees, killing them in the process. Using this wood helps to stop healthy trees from being cut down for construction materials.

🍁 **CANADIAN TIDBIT** The 2010 Games are estimated to cost more than $4 billion, including about $2.5 billion of taxpayer money.

Obstacle Course

Paralympic athletes compete at a high level. Athletes are visually impaired, have spinal cord injuries, are amputees, or have diseases such as cerebral palsy. Imagine what it would be like to compete in a sport without all of your physical abilities. Try this activity to test what it might be like to race without the use of your eyesight.

What you need

blindfold, obstacles, such as swimming pool noodles, hula hoops, and pylons, a friend

1. Use the obstacles to set up a course.

2. Cover your friend's eyes with the blindfold.

3. Guide your friend through the obstacle course. Be sure to tell this person when to step over, turn, walk around, or crawl through the obstacles on the course.

4. Now, trade places, and have your friend guide you through the course.

Further Research

Visit Your Library

Many books and websites provide information on the Paralympics. To learn more about the Paralympics, borrow books from the library, or surf the Internet.

Most libraries have computers that connect to a database for researching information. If you input a key word, you will be provided with a list of books in the library that contain information on that topic. Nonfiction books are arranged numerically, using their call number. Fiction books are organized alphabetically by the author's last name.

Surf the Web

Learn more about the Paralympics by visiting **www.paralympic.org**.

To learn more about the 2010 Paralympics in Vancouver, visit **www.vancouver2010.com**.

Glossary

aerobics: exercise for the heart and lungs

amputees: people who have had a part of their body removed

biathlon: a sport in which athletes combine cross-country skiing and target shooting skills

calories: units of energy, especially in food

cerebral palsy: a condition that typically causes impaired muscle coordination

core: the trunk of the body, including the hips and torso

discus: a sport in which athletes throw a disc as far as possible

endurance: the ability to continue doing something that is difficult

greenhouse gases: gases that are trapped within Earth's atmosphere, causing the greenhouse effect

heart rate: the number of times the heart beats in one minute

hybrid: a vehicle that uses a combination of fuels

intellectual disability: a disability that hampers the function of the mind

iron: a substance in foods that is good for the blood

javelin: a sport in which athletes throw a spear, or javelin, as far as they can

mechanical advantage: the ratio of the force produced by a machine to the force applied to it

medicine balls: weighted balls used in exercise regimens

pentathlon: a track and field competition that combines 10 different events

perseverance: a commitment to doing a task despite challenges that arise in the process

prostheses: artificial arms and legs

protein: a substance needed by the body to build healthy muscles

rehabilitation: working to recover from an injury

slide boards: a board athletes slide from side to side on in order to train their leg muscles

spinal cord: a bundle of nerves held inside the spine, connecting almost all parts of the body to the brain

sponsors: companies that help athletes by giving them merchandise or living expenses

stability balls: large rubber balls that athletes use to help with balance when they train

stamina: the ability to work hard for a long period of time

suspension: a system of springs and shock absorbers that provide cushioning

visually impaired: not being able to see well

Index